ALSO BY CHARLES WRIGHT

A Short History of the Shadow

....

A Short History of the Shadow

....

CHARLES WRIGHT

....

Farrar Straus Giroux

New York

Farrar, Straus and Giroux
19 Union Square West, New York 10003

Grateful acknowledgment is made to the editors of the following magazines,
in whose pages these poems originally appeared: *Poetry, The Bellingham Review,
The Getty Museum, Thumbscrew, Washington Square, Literary Imagination,
Meridian, Five Points, The Yale Review, St. Luke's Review, The Ohio Review, Field,
The New Yorker, PN Review, The Oxford American, Euphony, The New Republic,
Firefly, Ploughshares, 64 Magazine.*

The work in the second section, "Millennium Blues," was supported,
in part, by a grant from the Marion Center, College of Santa Fe,
for the project National Millennium Survey.

Library of Congress Cataloging-in-Publication Data
Wright, Charles, 1935–
    A short history of the shadow / Charles Wright.— 1st ed.
    p.   cm.
    ISBN 0-374-26302-7 (hardcover : alk. paper)
    I. Title.

PS3573.R52 S56 2002
811'.54—dc21

2001053255

Designed by Dorothy Schmiderer Baker

www.fsgbooks.com

1   3   5   7   9   10   8   6   4   2

For J.G., faith and friendship over the years

CONTENTS

....

RELICS

BODY AND SOUL

LOOKING AROUND

LOOKING AROUND

I sit where I always sit, in back of the Buddha,
Red leather wing chair, pony skin trunk
                              under my feet,
Skylight above me, Chinese and Indian rugs on the floor.
1 March, 1998, where to begin again?

Over there's the ur-photograph,
                Giorgio Morandi, glasses pushed up on his forehead,
Looking hard at four objects—
Two olive oil tins, one wine bottle, one flower vase,
A universe of form and structure,

The universe constricting in front of his eyes,
                              angelic orders
And applications scraped down
To paint on an easel stand, some in the frame, some not.
Bologna, my friend, Bologna, world's bite and world's end.

                ....

It's only in darkness you can see the light, only
From emptiness that things start to fill,
I read once in a dream, I read in a book
                              under the pink
Redundancies of the spring peach trees.

Old fires, old geographies.
In that case, make it old, I say, make it singular
In its next resurrection,
White violets like photographs on the tombstone of the yard.

3

Each year it happens this way, each year
Something dead comes back and lifts up its arms,
                                        puts down its luggage
And says—in the same costume, down-at-heels, badly sewn—
I bring you good news from the other world.

                    ....

One hand on the sun, one hand on the moon, both feet bare,
God of the late
                    Mediterranean Renaissance
Breaststrokes across the heavens.
Easter, and all who've been otherwised peek from their shells,

Thunderheads gathering at the rear
                                        abyss of things,
Lightning, quick swizzle sticks, troubling the dark in-between.
You're everything that I'm not, they think,
I'll fly away, Lord, I'll fly away.

April's agnostic and nickel-plated and skin deep,
Glitter and bead-spangle, haute couture,
The world its runway, slink-step and glide.
Roll the stone slowly as it vogues and turns,
                                        roll the stone slowly.

                    ....

Well, that was a month ago. May now,
What's sure to arrive has since arrived and been replaced,
Snick-snack, lock and load, grey heart's bull's-eye,
A little noon music out of the trees,
                                        a sonatina in green.

Spring passes. Across the room, on the opposite wall,
A 19th-century photograph

Of the Roman arena in Verona. Inside,
                                    stone tiers and stone gate.
Over the outer portico, the ghost of Catullus at sky's end.

The morning and evening stars never meet,
                                    nor summer and spring:
Beauty has been my misfortune,
                    hard journey, uncomfortable resting place.
Whatever it is I have looked for
Is tiny, so tiny it can dance in the palm of my hand.

                    ....

This is the moment of our disregard—
                                    just after supper,
Unseasonable hail in huddles across the porch,
The dogs whimpering,
                    thunder and lightning eddying off toward the east,
Nothing to answer back to, nothing to dress us down.

Thus do we slide into our disbelief
                                    and disaffection,
Caught in the weeds and understory of our own lives,
Bad weather, bad dreams.
Proper attention is our refuge now, our perch and our praise.

So? So. The moon has its rain-ring auraed around it—
The more that we think we understand, the less we see,
Back yard becoming an obelisk
Of darkness into the sky,
                    no hieroglyphs, no words to the wise.

Pale sky and one star, pale star,
Twilight twisting down like a slow screw
Into the balsa wood of Saturday afternoon,
Late Saturday afternoon,
                              a solitary plane
Eating its way like a moth across the bolt of dusk
Hung like cheesecloth above us.

Ugo would love this, Ugo Foscolo,
                                     everything outline,
Crepuscular, still undewed,
Ugo, it's said, who never uttered a commonplace,
His soul transfixed by a cypress tree,
The twilight twisted into his heart,
Ugo, immortal, unleavened, when death gave him fame and rest.

                   ....

Tonight, however's, a different story,
                                  flat, uninterrupted sky,
Memorial Day,
Rain off, then back again, a
Second-hand light, dishcloth light, wrung out and almost gone.
9:30 p.m.,
Lightning bugs, three of them, in my neighbor's yard,
                                  leaping beyond the hedge.

What can I possibly see back here I haven't seen before?
Is landscape, like God, a Heraclitean river?
Is language a night flight and sea-change?

My father was born Victorian,
                        knee-pants and red ringlets,
Sepia photographs and desk drawers
Vanishing under my ghostly touch.

                    ....

I sit where I always sit,
                        knockoff Brown Jordan plastic chair,
East-facing, lingering late spring dusk,
Virginia privet and honeysuckle in full-blown bloom and too sweet,
Sky with its glazed look, and half-lidded.
And here's my bat back,
The world resettled and familiar, a self-wrung sigh.

César Vallejo, on nights like this,
His mind in a crash dive from Paris to South America,
Would look from the Luxembourg
                            Gardens or some rooftop
For the crack, the tiny crack,
In the east that separates one world from the next,
                                    this one from
That one I look for it too.

                    ....

Now into June, cloverheads tight, Seurating the yard,
This land-washed *jatte* fireflied and Corgied.
How sweet familiarity is,
With its known bird songs,
                        its known smudges.
Today, as Machado said, is every day and all days.
A little wind from the southwest, a little wind in the apple tree.

And dusk descending, or dusk rising,
Sky flat as a sheet, smooth as bedclothes on a dead woman's bed.

It's always this way at 9 p.m.,
Half moon like a cleaved ox wheel
In miniature,
Machado smooth as a night bird half-asleep in the gum tree.

....

Crepuscularum. The back yard etched in and scored by
Lack of light.
What's dark gets darker against the shrinking, twilit sky,
Hedgerow and hemlock and maple tree.
A couple of lightning bugs.
Dog bark and summer smell.

                         Mosquitos. The evening star.

Been rode hard and put up wet, someone said to me once
In Kalispell, meaning,
                I hope I'm being used for a higher good,
Or one I'm not aware of.
Dino Campana could have said that.
Said it and meant, Lord, that's it. And please turn off the light.
And he did.

LOOKING AROUND III

August. Cloud-forest Chinese Ming screen
Beyond the south meadow and up the attendant feeder hills.
No wind and a steady rain.
Raven squawk and swallow bank,
                              screen shift at meadow mouth.
I find I have nothing to say to any of this.

Northwest Montana under the summer's backlash and wet watch.
The tall marsh grass kneels to their bidding.
The waters of Basin Creek pucker their tiny lips,
                              their thousand tiny lips.
The clouds shatter and the clouds re-form.
I find I have nothing to say to any of this.

....

Osip Mandelstam, toward the end of his short, word-fiery life,
Said heaven was whole, and that flowers live forever.
He also said what's ahead of us is only someone's word—
We were born to escort the dead, and be escorted ourselves.
Down by the creek bank, the sound that the water makes is almost
    human.

Down by the creek bank, the water sound
Is almost like singing, a song in praise of itself.
The light, like a water spider, stretches across the backwash.
Under the big spruce at the channel's bend,
                              someone's name and dates
Mirror the sky, whose way, like Mandelstam's, was lost in the sky.

....

Last night like spider light webbed and still in the tall grass,
Twin fawns and a doe at the salt lick,
Hail-battered marigolds and delphinium against the cabin wall,
Coyote about to trot out
Behind the diversion ditch and head for his breakfast.

I don't understand how white clouds can cover the earth.
I don't understand how a line of verse can fall from the sky.
I don't understand how the meadow mouth
                                        opens and closes.
I don't understand why the water keeps saying yes, O, yes.
I don't understand the black lake that pools in my heart.

....

Late afternoon and long shadows across the deer ford,
Mt. Henry volcanic and hushed against the west sky and cloud clot.
Dante, according to Mandelstam,
Was not descriptive, was never descriptive, his similes
Exposing the inner image of the structure's force—

Birds were a pilgrimage, for instance, rivers political.
Cloud and cloud-flow having their way,
                                        cloud-rags and cloud-rugs
Inching across the upper meadow, now the lower.
Inside the image inside the image is the image, he might have added,
Crystalline, pristine. But he didn't.

....

I sit where I always sit,
                    northwest window on Basin Creek,
A homestead cabin from 1912,
Pine table knocked together some 30 years ago,
Indian saddle blanket, Peruvian bedspread

And Mykonos woven rug
                    nailed up on the log walls.

Whose childhood is this in little rectangles over the chair?
Two kids with a stringer of sunfish,
Two kids in their bathing suits,
                            the short shadows of evergreens?
Under the meadow's summer coat, forgotten bones have turned black.
O, not again, goes the sour song of the just resurrected.

                    ....

To look hard at something, to look through it, is to transform it,
Convert it into something beyond itself, to give it grace.
For over 30 years I've looked at this meadow and mountain landscape
Till it's become iconic and small
And sits, like a medieval traveller's triptych,
                            radiant in its disregard.

All morning the donors have knelt, in profile, where the creeks meet,
The thin spruce have listened to what the rustle is, and nodded—
Like coyote's ears, they're split in the wind.
Tonight, after 10 p.m., the moon will varnish everything
With a brilliance worthy, wherever that is, of Paradise.

MILLENNIUM BLUES

....

CITRONELLA

Moonlight blank newsprint across the lawn,
Three-quarters moon, give or take,
                                empty notebook, no wind.
When it's over it's over,
Cloud crossing moon, half-clear sky, then
                                candle-sputter, shadow-crawl.

Well, that's a couple of miles down the road,
                                he said to himself,
Watching the moonlight lacquer and mat.
Surely a mile and then some,
Watching the clouds come and the clouds go.

Citronella against the tiny ones, the biters,
Sky pewter-colored and suddenly indistinct now—
Sweet smell of citronella,
                                beautiful, endless youth.
The book of moonlight has two pages and this one's the first one.

Forsake me not utterly,
Beato immaculato,
                and make me marvellous in your eyes.

IF THIS IS WHERE GOD'S AT, WHY IS THAT FISH DEAD?

If God is the one and infinite,
If God is the clear-cut and cloudless sky,

                      Powers, Dominions,

If God is a bed and a held breath,
You have a reason, my friend, to be inquisitive.

The morning smells like Milan, autumnal Milan, fog
And a fine rain in the trees,

                      huge plane leaves stuck on the sidewalks

Throughout the Sforza gardens,
Villa Guastalla calm as a ship

                through the part-brown park and the mist.

The Japanese say we live in twelve pictures thrown from the floating world,
Where sin is a ladder to heaven.

                    Or has been. Or can be.

First light in the east last light in the west and us in between,
Lives marginal at best

                and marginally brought to bear.

But that's okay, given the star-struck alternative.
Remember us in the ghost hour remember us in our need.

CHARLOTTESVILLE NOCTURNE

The late September night is a train of thought, a wound
That doesn't bleed, dead grass that's still green,
No off-shoots, no elegance,
                                    the late September night,
Deprived of adjectives, abstraction's utmost and gleam.

It has been said there is an end to the giving out of names.
It has been said that everything that's written has grown hollow.
It has been said that scorpions dance where language falters and gives way.
It has been said that something shines out from every darkness,
                                    that something shines out.

Leaning against the invisible, we bend and nod.
Evening arranges itself around the fallen leaves
Alphabetized across the back yard,
                                    desolate syllables
That braille us and sign us, leaning against the invisible.

Our dreams are luminous, a cast fire upon the world.
Morning arrives and that's it.
                        Sunlight darkens the earth.

IT'S DRY FOR SURE,

DRY ENOUGH TO SPIT COTTON

Afternoon, summer half-gone, autumn half-here, strange day,
Most of the grass dead, blue-grey cloud shelf
Thickening down from the west,
                                                    yard light
Like the inside of a diving bell not yet in deep water.

The afternoon's got our number.
                                        If only the rain
Would come and wash it off our foreheads.
If only the rain would come, unstrung through the hard weeds,
And wash us—sprung syllables, little eternities,

The rain with its thick fingers, the rain which will fill us
As slowly as hair grows, as slowly as fingernails—
Immaculate as the Jordan, Lord, Giovanni Battista
Out of the hills, hands faith-faint,
                                        huge as all nothingness.

Where the sky disappears, the horizon spurts like a needle.
We all have death's birthmark on our faces,
                                        sometimes red, sometimes unseeable.

IF MY GLASSES WERE BETTER,

I COULD SEE WHERE I'M HEADED FOR

Autumn is over us, leaf blowers
Whine in the wind, vans wail, the heart makes scurrying sounds
As though preparing itself to start out on a long journey.
It wants to carry us with it, safe in its damp folds.
It wants to carry us, one by one.

Birds split and the ants go south.
The weevils turn in their sleep inside the red doors of the trunk.
Housefly and bumblebee carcasses drain in the sun.
Words stuttered by hand.
                    Gates of mercy.
                                    Time after time.

As for me,
                I'll put on the pilgrim slippers some of these days
There, where all things are forgot.
Till then, I'll see that the grass gets mowed.
Till then, I'll check out the cloud's drift, and the season's drift,
And how the days move, one at a time,
                        always at night, and always in my direction.

LOST LANGUAGE

October, and leaves fall down. One feels the world go by.
First frost. And a licking sound
Just under the earth,
                    great wheels, or a sluice of some sort.
Sunlight thin as Saran Wrap.
A licking sound, the suck and bump of something against something.

One lives one's life in the word,
One word and a syllable, word and one syllable.
As though ice and its amulets could rise and rest us.
Whatever it is we look for is scattered, apart.

I have a thirst for the divine,
                    a long drink of forbidden water.
I have a hankering for the dust-light, for all things illegible.
I want to settle myself
Where the river falls on hard rocks,
                    where no one can cross,
Where the star-shadowed, star-colored city lies, just out of reach.

ON HEAVEN CONSIDERED AS WHAT WILL

COVER US AND STONY COMFORTER

The longed-for is tiny, and tenuous as a syllable.
In this it resembles us.
In this it resembles what we've passed on and shucked off.
Interminable as black water,
Irreparable as dirt,
It shadows our going forth and finds us,
                                     and then finds us out.

Horizon line like a basted
                         slipstitch that shines back,
Seasonal underwork, seasonal blueprint and burn.

Last stop. End of the end. No exit.
Autumn in override,
                    everyone long gone from the garden,
No footprints, wings furled, swords sheathed.
No gears, no wheels. A silence unimaginable.
Saint Sunday, leaves in free-fall,
A little light in the west, a night light,
                                   to harry us home.

MILDLY DEPRESSED, FAR FROM HOME,

I GO OUTSIDE FOR A WHILE

Bare yard trees, bare story line,
Unseasonable season,
                new moon
Diving hard right with the old moon stuck like a stone in her throat,
Down to November's 5 o'clock dingle and dark blue,
Sly script-bearer, silly fish,
Buried beneath our being like a splinter unlodgeable.

Starry night, cold stars of memory
Like floe tips on the black river.
                      How wide the world was,
How sweet the Orphean song,
How close the trees were then to the eddies of heaven.
I have taken my ease here long enough,
                        late autumn,
Late middle age, what am I waiting for?

May that which is dear to me come back,
                          and come back unto me,
Now boundless, now inexpressible.

MONDO ORFEO

Three-quarters moon, last of November,
                              5 o'clock afternoon.
Acolytes of the tactile, servants of the articulate,
The infinite festers in our bones—
Sundown, and a drained blue from the sky so long,
                              ghost whispers, lost voices,
Dry wind in dry grass, our bitter song.

Our song resettles no rocks, it makes no trees move, it
Has come to nothing, this sour song, but it's all we've got
And so we sing it
                    being ourselves
Matter we have no choice in.
Zone wind, wind out of Thrace were we elsewhere, which we're not,

But would be, oak trees still standing where he left them, Orpheus,
Whose head-bobbing river tongue has no stop,
                              whose song has no end.

For us, however, it's box canyon and bad weather and what-comes-next.
It's wind-rasp.
          It's index finger to puckered lips. It's Saint Shush.

THE SECRET OF POETRY

The second Chinese said, all that you need to find poetry
Is to look for it with a lantern.
Tonight, one night after full, the full moon feminine
Is all you would need,
The lunar essence, the blind structure of matter,

          perfection of pain,
Discharging unwilled and processional across the landscape.

Snow, and snow and ice, and snow again,
Came yesterday, before the moonlight.

         It's hard to find,
Despite what the Chinese said.
It's hard to find despite what the moonlight jukes and joins.
Now that the snow and ice have stopped, and the light's come back,
It hurts, and it's difficult to see.

The north wind in the bare limbs of the oak trees bears down on us.
The song of the north wind fills our ears with no meaning.

NIGHT MUSIC

....

IN PRAISE OF THOMAS HARDY

Each second the earth is struck hard
                    by four and a half pounds of sunlight.
Each second.
Try to imagine that.
                No wonder deep shade is what the soul longs for,
And not, as we always thought, the light.
No wonder the inner life is dark.
Sounding, and sicced on like a dog,
                                they all go down and devolve,
Vowel-dancing, heart-sick,
Hoping for realignment and a space that won't shine.

Unlike the October moon, Apached and blade-dazzled, smalled
Down the western sky
                    into Ovidian intersect
With time and its ghostly renderings.
Unlike the leaves of the ash tree, moon-treated and hanging on
For one day longer or so.
Unlike our shrunk selves, dripping like washing on the line.

Winter blue moon, light like a wax-thin slice of *finocchio*,
So grainy, so white.
It's 1999, last night of January,
Everything order and form out back, everything in its place
Ready for praise—which I give—in its ghost and disguise.

Still, something is calling us, something not unlike unbeing.
The lure of the incidental calls,
                              immensity beckons.
All who have turned from memory, all who have not turned,
One by one we are called,
                         one by one we are chosen—
The fire here is the fire there, ash, and the sure-fire end of ash.

O Something, be with me, time is short.
Our days are like slipped stitches,
                              the cloth is wide and deep.
Our prayers go unanswered, if prayers they are, our whispers unheard.
No earth, no heaven.
Thus are we summoned, we who have not understood this.

....

That which was broken away from you will be restored,
That which time took, that which earth borrowed, will be returned,
It says somewhere in a book.
It also says, the shadow of light is within us.
It also says, the tomb of the body is forgetfulness.

Not too much thought of endgame today, however, blue
Crack in the east, blue
                    crinkle and dip
Of Piedmont toward Tidewater,
Central Virginia suddenly sunlight and loose glass
As February's kaleidoscope turns once, then turns again.

But always, like the distant susurration of surf
Heard and half-heard in the burning ear—
I am the undefiled and incorruptible one;
I do not exist, as everything mortal exists in me,
Sunfall like water sheen in backwash across the yard.

                    ....

Nothing prepares the brain
                    for the heavy changes in the heart.
Nothing prepares the soul for metaphor's sleight-of-hand.
Nothing prepares the left hand—luminous twin—for the sins of the right.
Nothing prepares the absence of pain for the presence of pain.
Nothing prepares what is for what's not.

One gets tired.
The sun goes up and the sun goes down and one gets tired.
When evening comes, the doves will settle down in the holly tree,
The story goes. When evening comes,
                    the winds will be black,
And treetops, even without their leaves, will start to sway.

Meanwhile, let's tinker around some with the afternoon,
Its lack of smell, its half-broken and unmended trees,
Its text of appearances
                    that belies the world as we must read it,
Slowly now, uninterruptedly,
More shadow than light, more shade than dark on the clean page.

Moon partial tonight,
                a Tuscan bean in a non-Tuscan sky,
A promise of what's to come.
Not much to say to what is,
The dark almost absolute down here,
                         lack of familiar things,
A promise partially kept.

Even so, I think it's all incomprehensible,
Everything that we look at.
Much easier, I think, to imagine the abyss, just there,
The other side of the hedge,
                    than to conjure the hedge,
The trees, and time like a puddle of water and not a stream.

Below me, red-clay Rivanna, river of Lethe
I cross and re-cross each day.
The world, I think, was made by mistake.
                                Perishable, mortal,
It is like us, its children, pale and predictable.
Unlike the abyss, such black, such immortal water.

Still night, unholy night, dark of the moon,
                        pagan stars
A twice-splattered narrative
Retracked in their intervals like secret thoughts through the black sky.
We all have our ways of telling things,
Great chunks of dead flesh broken up into lines of poetry.

We all have our ways of keeping the Buddha alive
As he comes forth, a common pilgrim, out of the thick forest.
We all have our ways of directing the sacrificial horse

Back to the place of sacrifice,
                        as if he'd appeared
By chance, though guided, the Indians say, like Buddha imperceptibly.

And there's his arrangement in the sky.
And here's his arrangement on the ground,
                        pleasure of the without,
Brittle and secondary February bloom stalks,
Trees leafless and shadowless
Just under Orion, just west of the Pleiades.

                ....

Snuff end of February, no moon and
                        cold tongs to the touch,
Year of the Rabbit, 15 degrees.
Crunch, crunch goes grass like broken head hair,
Our breath like Apache smoke signals
                        —they come, they come—
From one yard to the next. But they don't come, Lord, they don't.

If I had, as Robert Johnson says, possession over Judgment Day,
No stone would rest unrisen,
And life, which promises only that we will desire
Only the things we can't have,
Would be rolled away,
                        cool dark of cave mouth first exit,

Crocus heads gazing quietly at the distant southern hills.
As one absorbed in looking around,
                        each time I've looked, each time it's new—
Each time I said it, I got it wrong.
In front of me, two plus two, behind me, two plus two.
If I could do what I thought I could do, I would leave no trace.

Transcendence is a young man's retreat,
                              and resides in a place
Beyond place, vasty, boundless.
It hums, unlike the beauty of the world,
                       without pause, without mercy.

If it's an absence, it's we who are absent, not it.
If it's past cold and colorless,
                         it's we who are colorless, not it.
If it stays hidden, it's we who hide.

March is our medicine,
                  we take it at morning, we take it at night.
It, too, is colorless, it, too, is cold and past tense.
But it's here, and so are we.

Each waits for deliverance.
March, however, unlike ourselves, knows what to expect—
April again in his Joseph coat.

The seasons don't care for us. For them,
                         transcendence is merely raiment,
And never a second thought.
Poor us, they think, poor us in our marly shoes,
                            poor us in our grass hair.

POLAROIDS

Since landscape's insoluble,
Then loath at last light I leave the landfall, soft and gone.
Or it leaves me.
                    I've got a tune in my head I can't let go,
Unlike the landscape, heavy and wan,
Sunk like a stone in the growing night,
Snuffed in the heart like a candle flame that won't come back.

Our world is of little moment, of course, but it *is* our world.
Thus it behooves us to contemplate,
                         from time to time,
The *weight of glory* we should wish reset in our hearts,
About the things which are seen,
                      and things which are not seen,
That corresponds like to like,
The stone to the dark of the earth, the flame to the star.

               ....

Those without stories are preordained to repeat them,
I saw once in the stars.
                  Unclear who underwrote *that*,
But since then I've seen it everywhere
I've looked, staggering
Noon light and night's meridian wandering wide and the single sky.
And here it is in the meadow grass, a brutish script.

We tend to repeat what we don't know
Instead of the other way around—
                       thus mojo, thus misericordia,

Old cross-work and signature, the catechism in the wind.
We tend to repeat what hurts us, things, and ghosts of things,
The actual green of summer, and summer's half-truth.
We tend to repeat ourselves.

....

One longs for order and permanence,
An order as in the night sky just north of Mt. Caribou,
Permanence like the seasons,
                                   coming in, going out,
Watchman and wanderer. There's been no cure, however, and no
Ecstasy in transcendent form, so
Don't look for me here, incipient, now, in the artifice.

Florence is much on my mind, gold leaf and golden frame,
Infinite background of the masters—
Mayfire of green in the hills,
                                   watchtower and Belvedere,
The Arno, as Dino said, like a dithering snake,
Sad swipe of forgetfulness.
Last chance, a various universe.

....

A few more rising and setting suns.
Always the spike of the purple lupin, always the folded hands of the
    dog rose.
Childhood, gentle monk.
His eye extinguished,
                                   someone's red-gold heart-mouth has sealed his lips.
No wind in the evergreens, no singer, no lament.
Summer surrounds us, and wordless, O blue cathedral.

A few more sorrowful scenes.
The waters murmur, shadows are moist in the upper meadow.

Silence wide as a wasteland through the black streets of the forest.
Over the white eyelids of the dead,
                                      white clover is blossoming.
Late snow like a fallen city shimmers the mountain's riprap and stare.
Unmullioned window, stained light.

                        ....

The lapis lazuli dragonflies
                            of postbelief, rising and falling near
The broken slab wood steps, now one by one, now in pairs,
Are not the dragonflies of death with their blue-black eyes.
These are the tiny ones, the stems, the phosphorescent,
Rising and falling like drowned playthings.
They come and they disappear. They come back and they disappear.

Horizon-hump of pine bristles on end toward the south,
Breath-stealer, cloudless drop cloth
Of sky,
        the great meadow beneath like a mirror face down in the earth,
Accepting nothing, giving it back.
We'll go, as Mandelstam tells us, into a growing numbness of time,
Insoluble, as long as landscape, as indistinct.

NOSTALGIA

Always it comes when we least expect it, like a wave,
Or like the shadow of several waves,
                                        one after the next,
Becoming singular as the face

Of someone who rose and fell apart at the edge of our lives.

Breaks up and re-forms, breaks up, re-forms.
And all the attendant retinue of loss foams out
Brilliant and sea-white, then sinks away.

Memory's dog-teeth,
                    lovely detritus smoothed out and laid up.

And always the feeling comes that it was better then,
Whatever *it* was—
                    people and places, the sweet taste of things—
And this one, wave-borne and wave-washed, was part of all that.

We take the conceit in hand, and rub it for good luck.

Or rub it against the evil eye.
And yet, when that wave appears, or that wave's shadow, we like it,
Or say we do,
                and hope the next time

We'll be surprised again, and returned again, despite the fact

The time will come, they say, when the weight of nostalgia,
                                        that ten-foot spread
Of sand in the heart, outweighs
Whatever living existence we drop on the scales.

May it never arrive, Lord, may it never arrive.

A SHORT HISTORY OF THE SHADOW

Thanksgiving, dark of the moon.
Nothing down here in the underworld but vague shapes and black holes,
Heaven resplendent but virtual
Above me,
              trees stripped and triple-wired like Irish harps.
Lights on Pantops and Free Bridge mirror the eastern sky.
Under the bridge is the river,
                  the red Rivanna.
Under the river's redemption, it says in the book,
It says in the book,
Through water and fire the whole place becomes purified,
The visible by the visible, the hidden by what is hidden.

            ....

Each word, as someone once wrote, contains the universe.
The visible carries all the invisible on its back.
Tonight, in the unconditional, what moves in the long-limbed grasses,
                        what touches me
As though I didn't exist?
What is it that keeps on moving,
                a tiny pillar of smoke
Erect on its hind legs,
              loose in the hollow grasses?
A word I don't know yet, a little word, containing infinity,
Noiseless and unrepentant, in sift through the dry grass.
Under the tongue is the utterance.
Under the utterance is the fire, and then the only end of fire.

            ....

Only Dante, in Purgatory, casts a shadow,
L'ombra della carne, the shadow of flesh—

                                      everyone else *is* one.
The darkness that flows from the world's body, gloomy spot,
Pre-dogs our footsteps, and follows us,

                                diaphanous bodies
Watching the nouns circle, and watching the verbs circle,
Till one of them enters the left ear and becomes a shadow
Itself, sweet word in the unwaxed ear.
This is a short history of the shadow, one part of us that's real.
This is the way the world looks
In late November,

         no leaves on the trees, no ledge to foil the lightfall.

                  ....

No ledge in early December either, and no ice,
La Niña unhosing the heat pump

                         up from the Gulf,
Orange Crush sunset over the Blue Ridge,
No shadow from anything as evening gathers its objects
And eases into earshot.
Under the influx the outtake,

                    Leon Battista Alberti says,
Some lights are from stars, some from the sun
And moon, and other lights are from fires.
The light from the stars makes the shadow equal to the body.
Light from fire makes it greater,

            there, under the tongue, there, under the utterance.

RIVER RUN

In spite of armchair and omelette,
In spite of the daily paradise and quid pro quo,
Like Lorca, I wait for
                                    the things of the other side,
A little river of come and go,
A heartbeat of sorts, a watch tick, a splash in the night.

Wherever I turn, everything looks unworldly
Already,
                    the stars in their empty boxes, the lights
Of the high houses glowing like stones
Through the thrones of the trees,
                                    the river hushed in a brown study.

What isn't available is always what's longed for,
It's written, erased, then written again.
                                    Thus Lost and Unknown,
Thus Master of the Undeciphered Parchment, thus Hail and Farewell.
It's not the bullet that kills you, as the song goes,
                                    it's the hole.
It's not the water you've got to cross, it's the river.

APPALACHIAN LULLABY

In Kingsport, high on the ridge,
                    night is seeping out of the Cumberlands
And two-steps the hills, shadows in ecstasy across the sky—
Not dark, not dark, but almost,
                    deep and a sweet repose.

Under the washed-red mimosa spikes,
                    under the blue backwash
Of evening, under the gun
Of mother-prayer and expectation, gently the eyelids close.

My sister and mother and father, each
In a separate room,
     stay locked in a private music and drift away, night
And day, drift away.

I hear the gates of my life snick shut,
Air kisses,
     kisses from some place that I've never been, but will be from.
Snick snick through the Red Sea, snick snick toward the promised land.

Someone is turning the lights out.
                    The darkness is mine,
Time, slow liquid, like a black highway in front of me
Somewhere, no headlights, somewhere.

Hello goodbye hello. Works and days.
We come, we hang out, we disappear.

There are stars above us that can't be counted,
                             and can't be counted on.

Gently the eyelids close.
                    Not dark, not dark. But almost.
Drift away. And drift away.
A deep and a sweet repose.

I think of the nightfall all the time.
I think of the dark pine trees
                                leaning out of the sky
Backlit by diminishing twilight, then not backlit.
I think of the way the tree frogs pitch
And pull in their summer dance.
I think of how the wind comes in from thousands of miles away.
I think of how the darkness abides.

The world's a slick rock we've got to cross,
The air, as Cavalcanti says, tremulous with light
And everywhere nicked with voices and little outcries.
Whose are they, and who are they,
                                their wings horizon edged,
Their bodies as soft as clouds, their skins tattooed and laid bare and
Graffitied with desolation?
Dreams of them enter, like things alive, the rooms where our loves lie
    sleeping.

Listen to what the book says—
Woe to you because of the fire that burns in you, for it is insatiable.
Woe to you because of the wheel that turns in your mind.
This is the way the night comes on,
                                a narrow and shapeless place,
A few rehearsals among the insects, a few stars,
The thing invisible brought to naught, and back among visible things.
This is the way it all ends.

RELICS

....

THINKING OF WALLACE STEVENS AT
THE BEGINNING OF SPRING

There is so much that clings to us, and wants to keep warm.
Familiar things—the blue sky,
Spring sun,
    some dark musician chording the sacred harp,
His spittle of notes
Pressed violets in his still darker book of revelation.

Why do they stay so cold, why
Do the words we give them disguise their identity
As abject weather,
    perverse descriptions, inordinate scales?
The poem is virga, a rain that never falls to earth.
That's why we look this way, our palms outstretched,
      our faces jacked toward the blue.

RELICS

After a time, Hoss, it makes such little difference
What anyone writes—
Relics, it seems, of the thing
                              are always stronger than the thing itself.
Palimpsest and pentimento, for instance, saint's bones
Or saint's blood,
Transcendent architecture of what was possible, say,
                                                  once upon a time.

The dogwoods bloom, the pink ones and the white ones, in blots
And splotches across the dusk.
                              Like clouds, perhaps. Mock clouds
In a mock heaven,
The faint odor of something unworldly, or otherworldly,
Lingering in the darkness, then not.
As though some saint had passed by the side yard,
                              the odor of Paradise,

As Aldo Buzzi has it,
Odor of Heaven, the faithful say.
And what is this odor like? someone who'd smelled it was asked once.
He had no answer, and said,
"It doesn't resemble any flower or any bloom or spice on this earth.
I wouldn't know how to describe it."
                              Lingering as the dark comes on.

St. Gaspare Del Bufalo was one of these fragrant saints,
Buzzi continues,

St. Gaspare, who walked in the rain without an umbrella and still stayed
    dry.
Miraculous gift.
He knew, he added, one of the saint's relatives, a pianist,
                        who served him an osso buco once
In a penthouse in Milan.

Let's see. A cold spring in Charlottesville,
End of April, 2000—
If you can't say what you've got to say in three lines,
                        better change your style.
Nobody's born redeemed, nobody's moonlight, golden fuse in the
    deadly trees.
White wind through black wires,
                      humming a speech we do not speak.
Listen for us in the dark hours, listen for us in our need.

WHY, IT'S AS PRETTY AS A PICTURE

A shallow thinker, I'm tuned
                to the music of things,
The conversation of birds in the dusk-damaged trees,
The just-cut grass in its chalky moans,
The disputations of dogs, night traffic, I'm all ears
To all this and half again.

And so I like it out here,
Late spring, off-colors but firming up, at ease among half things.
At ease because there is no overwhelming design
                        I'm sad heir to,
At ease because the dark music of what surrounds me
Plays to my misconceptions, and pricks me, and plays on.

It is a kind of believing without belief that we believe in,
This landscape that goes
               no deeper than the eye, and poises like
A postcard in front of us
As though we'd settled it there, just so,
Halfway between the mind's eye and the mind, just halfway.

And yet we tend to think of it otherwise. Tonight,
For instance, the wind and the mountains and half-moon talk
Of unfamiliar things in a low familiar voice,
As though their words, however small, were putting the world in place.
And they are, they are,
              the place inside the place inside the place.

The postcard's just how we see it, and not how it is.
Behind the eye's the other eye,
                              and the other ear.
The moonlight whispers in it, the mountains imprint upon it,
Our eyelids close over it,
Dawn and the sunset radiate from it like Eden.

NINE-PANEL YAAK RIVER SCREEN

Midmorning like a deserted room, apparition
Of armoire and table weights,
Oblongs of flat light,
                    the rosy eyelids of lovers
Raised in their ghostly insurrection,
Decay in the compassed corners beating its black wings,
Late June and the lilac just ajar.

Where the deer trail sinks down through the shadows of blue spruce,
Reeds rustle and bow their heads,
Creek waters murmur on like the lamentation of women
For faded, forgotten things.
And always the black birds in the trees,
Always the ancient chambers thudding inside the heart.

                 ....

Swallow pure as a penknife
                    slick through the insected air.
Swallow poised on the housepost, beakful of mud and a short straw.
Swallow dun-orange, swallow blue,
                    mud purse and middle arch,
Home sweet home.
Swallow unceasing, swallow unstill
At sundown, the mother's shade over silver water.

At the edge of the forest, no sound in the grey stone,
No moan from the blue lupin.
The shadows of afternoon
                    begin to gather their dark robes

And unlid their crystal eyes.
Minute by minute, step by slow step,
Like the small hand on a clock, we climb north, toward midnight.

....

I've made a small hole in the silence, a tiny one,
Just big enough for a word.
And when I rise from the dead, whenever that is, I'll say it.
I can't remember the word right now,
But it will come back to me when the northwest wind
                                        blows down off Mt. Caribou
The day that I rise from the dead, whenever that is.

Sunlight, on one leg, limps out to the meadow and settles in.
Insects fall back inside their voices,
Little fanfares and muted repeats,
Inadequate language of sorrow,
                              inadequate language of silted joy,
As ours is.
The birds join in. The sunlight opens her other leg.

....

At times the world falls away from us
                              with all its disguises,
And we are left with ourselves
As though we were dead, or otherwised, our lips still moving,
The empty distance, the heart
Like a votive little-red-wagon on top of a child's grave,
Nothing touching, nothing close.

A long afternoon, and a long rain begins to fall.
In some other poem, angels emerge from their cold rooms,
Their wings blackened by somebody's dream.

The rain stops, the robin resumes his post.

                                        A whisper
Out of the clouds and here comes the sun.
A long afternoon, the robin flying from post back to post.

                    ....

The length of vowel sounds, by nature and by position,
Count out the morning's meters—
                                birdsong and squirrel bark, creek run,
The housefly's languor and murmurous incantation.
I put on my lavish robes
And walk at random among the day's
                                        dactyls and anapests,
A widening caesura with each step.

I walk through my life as though I were a bookmark, a holder of place,
An overnight interruption
                            in somebody else's narrative.
What is it that causes this?
What is it that pulls my feet down, and keeps on keeping my eyes
                                        fixed to the ground?
Whatever the answer, it will start
                            the wolf pack down from the mountain,
The raven down from the tree.

                    ....

Time gnaws on our necks like a dog
                            gnaws on a stew bone.
It whittles us down with its white teeth,
It sends us packing, leaving no footprints on the dust-dour road.
That's one way of putting it.
Time, like a golden coin, lies on our tongue's another.
We slide it between our teeth on the black water,
                                        ready for what's next.

The white eyelids of dead boys, like flushed birds, flutter up
At the edge of the timber.
Domestic lupin Crayolas the yard.
                                        Slow lopes of tall grasses
Southbound in the meadow, hurled along by the wind.
In wingbeats and increments,
The disappeared come back to us, the soul returns to the tree.

                        ....

The intermittent fugues of the creek,
                                saying yes, saying no,
Master music of sunlight
And black-green darkness under the spruce and tamaracks,
Lull us and take our breath away.
                                Our lips form fine words,
But nothing comes out.
Our lips are the messengers, but nothing can come out.

After a day of high winds, how beautiful is the stillness of dusk.
Enormous silence of stones.
Illusion, like an empty coffin, that something is missing.
Monotonous psalm of underbrush
                                and smudged flowers.
After the twilight, darkness.
After the darkness, darkness, and then what follows that.

                        ....

The unborn own all of this, what little we leave them,
St. Thomas's hand
                        returning repeatedly to the wound,
Their half-formed mouths irrepressible in their half-sleep,
Asking for everything, and then some.
Already the melancholy of their arrival

Swells like a sunrise and daydream
                                        over the eastern ridge line.

Inside the pyrite corridors of late afternoon,
Image follows image, clouds
Reveal themselves,
        and shadows, like angels, lie at the feet of all things.
Chambers of the afterlife open deep in the woods,
Their secret hieroglyphics suddenly readable
With one eye closed, then with the other.

                    ....

One star and a black voyage,
                            drifting mists to wish on,
Bullbats and their lullaby—
Evening tightens like an elastic around the hills.
Small sounds and the close of day,
As if a corpse had risen from somewhere deep in the meadow
And walked in its shadows quietly.

The mouth inside me with its gold teeth
Begins to open.
No words appear on its lips,
                            no syllables bubble along its tongue.
Night mouth, silent mouth.
Like drugged birds in the trees,
                        angels with damp foreheads settle down.
Wind rises, clouds arrive, another night without stars.

THE WIND IS CALM AND COMES
FROM ANOTHER WORLD

Overcast August morning.
                              A little rain in the potholes,
A little shade on the shade.
The world is unconversational, and bides its own sweet time.
What you see is what you see, it seems to say, but we
Know better than that,
                    and keep our eyes on the X, the cloud-ridden sky.

Heliotrope, we say, massaging its wings. Heliotrope.

SUMMER MORNINGS

Over the hill, the river's glib.
                                    In multiple tongues,
It's got a line of talk for anyone who wants it.
Lonely summer morning. Dwarf willows,
Black corners, a safe shadow for anyone who wants it.

What the river says isn't enough.
The scars of unknowing are on our cheeks,
                                    those blank pages.
I'll let the wind speak my piece.
I'll let the Vocalissimo lay me down,
                                    and no one else.

                    ....

There is out here, on summer mornings, a kind of light,
                                    silky and rare,
That drapes through the evergreens
Every so often when clouds from the northwest glacier across
The sun and disintegrate.

A light like the absence of light it is so feral and shy.
A pentimento, even.
It is as though it dreamed us out of its solitude.
It is as though we're glazed here,
                                    unasked for, unremembering.

                    ....

It's Monday back there in the land of the Chickasaws.
The white clouds stumble upon each other, and pile up

Like mountains of faithlessness,
As clouds will, on a summer morning,
                              forgetting nothing, as clouds do.

Bright Monday. Unbearable light in the evergreens.
Dark river beneath it,
                    threading the eye of the underworld.
Above, on the great current of air,
The clouds drift on to their appointed stations, as clouds will do.

....

Odor of propane, nervous rustling of aspen leaves,
Summer morning unravelling silently through the woods.
The long body of the Hunter Gracchus sails by on its black water.
Late, golden July.

Time, like a swallow's shadow cutting across the grass,
Faint, darker, then faint again,
Imprints our ecstasy, and scores us.
And time will finish this, not I, and write it out,
                              as only time can.

....

The river rises in the mind, but empties nowhere,
Its hair naked in naked branches.
Spiders swing through my heart,
                      the moons of Jupiter turn and shine,
The river slides on its flaming wheel

And sings on summer mornings,
                      as though to croon itself to sleep.
And mumbles a kind of nothingness,
River that flows everywhere, north and south, like the wind
And never closes its eye.

Cloud skiff, like early snowfall, on the move from the west
Over Mt. Henry and my shoulder.
St. Pablo, patron of horses, appears through his wounds.
Hoofprints in khaki-colored dust.

> Horseman salve our sins.

Summer morning. Gun-grey sky.
Rust keeps nibbling away at the edges of our lives.
Under the roots of the pine trees,

> under the thunder,

Lightning is tracking our footprints, one leg at a time.

....

Bird life. An unappeasable bird life.
Saint's flesh melting into the flames below the brazier.
Sky flat and blank as parchment,
Wordless, encrypted blue,

> God's endgame, summer morning.

The secret language of butterflies.
The short shadows of those

> who will not rise from the dead.

The broken dream-cries of angels half-dazed in the woods.
The adjective and the noun.

THINKING OF MARSILIO FICINO AT
THE FIRST HINT OF AUTUMN

We yo-yo the Absolute big-time,
Dark little spinning thing.
                              Still, death is the deeper exile and
Waits for our fancy—
Its business is process, and hiding out, and keeping in touch,
Tenth night in a row of rain,
Black as an owl's eye,
Thunder and lightning out of the West Virginia mountains like God's yips
And hotfoots,
                 trees processional maidens dipping in turn,
Cold front from the north
Pinning our ears back, shorting our breath.

Last night and a world away.
This afternoon like a waffle, indented and warm,
Delicious and blue on the tongue,
                                    early September.
Ficino, however, is probably right, the Absolute
Not being an exile but a grace,
And waits for no one,
                         the way, this afternoon, the sun
Kindles and plumps the dogwood berries,
The way the individual necks in the cutting garden
Bow dutifully to what's to come,
The way Orion and the Pleiades
                                 rise up, ready to go on.

VIA NEGATIVA

....

If a man wants to be sure of his road,
he must close his eyes and walk in the dark.

ST. JOHN OF THE CROSS

In Southwest Virginia, just this side of Abingdon,
The mountains begin to shoulder up,
The dogwoods go red and leaf-darkened,
And leftover roadside wildflowers neon among the greens—
Early October, and Appalachia dyes her hair.
What is it about the southern mountains

                        that vacuums me out,
That seems to hold me on an invisible flame until I rise up and veer
weightless and unrepentant?
The great valley pours into Tennessee, the ridges like epaulets
To the north, landscape in pinks-and-greens

                                off to the south.

               ....

How pretty to think that gods abound,

                      and everything stays forgotten,
That words are dust, and everyone's lip that uttered them is dust,
Our line of discomfort inalterable, sun-struck,
From not-ness into not-ness,
Our prayers—like raiment, like char scraps—rising without us
Into an everlasting,

                 which goes on without us,
Blue into blue into blue—
Our prayers, like wet-wrung pieces of glass,
Surf-spun, unedged and indestructible and shining,

Our lives a scratch on the sky,
                    painless, beyond recall.

                    ....

I never remember going out at night, full moon,
Stalking the yard in California the way I do here,
First frost
                    starting to sort its crystals out, moon shadows
Tepid and underslung on the lawn.
I don't remember—although I should—the emptiness
That cold brings, and stillness brings.
I never remember remembering the odd way
Evergreens have in night light
                    of looming and floating,
The way the spirit, leaving your mouth, looms too and floats
In front of you like breath,
                    leading the way as it disappears in the darkness.

                    ....

Long journey, short road, the saying goes,
Meaning our lives,
                    meaning the afterlife of our nights and days
During our sleepwalk through them.
The verbal hunger, the narrowness
Between the thing itself and the naming of the thing
Coils like a tapeworm inside us
                    and waits to be filled.
Our lives continue on course, and reject all meaning,
Each of us needing his martyrdom,
                    each of us needing that hard love.
We sink to our knees like Sunday, we rise and we sink again.
There is no pardon for this.

                    ....

Bottomless water, heart's glass.
Each year the autumn comes that was not supposed to be
Back in the garden without language,
Each year, dead leaves like words
                                falling about our shoulders,
Each year, same words, same flash and gold guise.
So be it. The Angel of the Serpent That Never Arrives
Never arrives, the gates stay shut
                                under a shine and a timelessness.
On Locust Avenue the fall's fire
Collapses across the lawn,
The trees bear up their ruin,
                and everything nudges our lives toward the coming ash.

November in cameo, pink blink.
Four fingers, forsworn from their hand,
                                        pick up their burden
And tap out the messages day-after-tomorrow licks up,
Sidereal tongue.
Gates of Mercy, stop breaking down.

Cloud strips like raw bacon slatted above the west edge of things,
Cold like a shot of Novocain
                                under the week's gums.
Thanksgiving Day, 2000.
Four insect hulls in the far corner,
                                fly inert on its back.
Inside or outside, a slow climb to the second life.

Rimbaud, at the end, had got it right—
Absurd, ridiculous, disgusting, etc.—
(Meaning his poems, meaning his life in literature)
But got the direction wrong.
                    That's not why you quit, but why you keep on,
Sky with its burners damped, husk and web.

What's lost is not lost, but purls
Just out of earshot.
                    Be bright, it murmurs. Be brighter.
Words foursquare and indestructible.
The River of Heaven. River Where Elephants Come to Die.
Old lights, old destinations.

Like clouds, our dead friends drift by,
                              white and off-white, long lengths.
Tap-tap, tap-tap-tap.
Their shadows harbor in us, their mouths motion us down.
Who knows what they have to say from the far side of the seasons,
Their end-mouths so blue, so blue.

'54 CHEVY

Sam's Gap, the Tennessee side,
Kiss-your-ass curve and white house on the poor field's aneurysm,
A handful of Alzheimered apple trees across the highway,
South Mountain back to the right,

Delicate short grasses, bird flocks in the trees, pasture
And cupped orchard
                                    green against the unendable blue
. Of North Carolina sky just over the hill.
                                                    And the heart,
That legless bird, circling and circling, hoping for anywhere to land.

A moment that should have lasted forever and forever
Long over—
                        it came and went before I knew it existed.
I think I know what it means,
But every time I start to explain it, I forget the words.

NOSTALGIA II

January, moth month,
                    crisp frost-flank and fluttering,
Verona,
Piazza Brà in the cut-light,
                    late afternoon, mid-winter,
1959,
Roman arena in close-up tonsured and monk robed
After the snowfall.

Behind my back, down via Mazzini, the bookstore
And long wooden table in whose drawer
Harold will show me, in a month or so,
                    the small books
From Vanni Scheiwiller, *All'insegna del pesce d'oro*,
That will change my life,
Facsimiles, *A Lume Spento*, and *Thrones*, full blown, in boards.

Made in Verona. Stamperia Valdonega.
That's how it all began, in my case,
                    Harold and I
Ghosting the bookstores and bars,
Looking for language and a place to stand that fit us,
The future, like Dostoevsky, poised
To read us the riot act.
                And it did. And it's been okay.

BODY AND SOUL

....

BODY AND SOUL

....

(*for Coleman Hawkins*)

The world's body is not our body,
                                            although we'd have it so.
Our body's not infinite, although
This afternoon, under the underwater slant-shine
Of sunlight and cloud shadow,
It almost seems that way in the wind,
                                            a wind that comes
From a world away with its sweet breath and its tart tongue
And casts us loose, like a cloud,
Heaven-ravaged, blue pocket, small change for the hand.

I used to think the power of words was inexhaustible,
That how we said the world
                                    was how it was, and how it would be.
I used to imagine that word-sway and word-thunder
Would silence the Silence and all that,
That words were the Word,
That language could lead us inexplicably to grace,
As though it were geographical.
I used to think these things when I was young.
                                            I still do.

Some poems exist still on the other side of our lives,
And shine out,
            but we'll never see them.
They are unutterable, in a language without an alphabet.
Unseen. World-long. Bone music.

Too bad. We'd know them by heart
                    if we could summer them out in our wounds.
Too bad. Listening hard.
Clouds, of course, are everywhere, and blue sky in between.
Blue sky. Then what comes after the blue.

Our lives, it turns out, are still-lifes, glass bottles and fruit,
Dead animals, flowers,
                    the edges of this and that
Which drop off, most often, to indeterminate vacancy.
We're beautiful, and hung up to dry.
                              Outside the frame,
Mountains are moving, rivers flash, a cloud-scrumbled sky.
Field-patches nudge up to comfort us.
A train crosses a trestle.
Across the room, someone gets up and rearranges the things.

Insubstantial as smoke, our words
Drum down like fingertips across the page,
                              leaving no smudge or mark.
Unlike our purloined selves, they will not rise from the dead.
Unlike our whimpers and prayers, they lie low and disappear.
This word, that word, all fall down.
How far from heaven the stars are,
                              how far the heart from the page.
We don't know what counts—
It's as simple as that, isn't it,
                    we just don't know what counts.

Mid-winter in Charlottesville,
                    soul-shunt and pat-down, crumbs
Snow-flecked across the back yard, then gone on the sun's tongue.
These are the four lessons I have learned,

One from Martha Graham,
                          three others from here and there—
Walk as though you'd been given one brown eye and one blue,
Think as though you thought best with somebody else's brain,
Write as though you had in hand the last pencil on earth,
Pray as though you were praying with someone else's soul.

HARD DREAMS

Night after tomorrow night,
Slingshot and backlit.
                Nightmemories, night outsourcings.
Little eternities. Languageless light syllables.
Now nightstone is rolled away. Forever gets longer.
Dawn squawks and cloud zoom. Eye blear.

Ephemera's what moves us,
                the see-through rooms, the house on stilts,
Vast unreachable destinations
Drifting on unwashed currents,
The shipwreck of spring inexorable, and on time,
One drop of blood in its left eye, one drop in the right.

Whatever was written goes shell-empty and shell-dark.
The beyond flicks on its lights.
That which has not been said remains unutterable.
Another winter afternoon in the underworld.
On the dead lawn grass, a single ear,
                    listening, listening.

In Caravaggio, for instance, there is a hard light
In the Maltese painting, *Beheading of St. John*,
                    right to left,
Which shows us that suffering's inexact, diffused, and without a sigh.
It goes on and it goes on
Like a nursery rhyme, like spring rain, like another nursery rhyme.

To walk on the snow without footprints,
To stride like a Jesus bug across the black water,
To part the wind like a hair,
To be as apprehensive as smoke,
To disappear like a current inside a river . . .

Who's to say if the angel wings that trouble our sleep
Are a paradise enough?
Who is to say if the endless and empty cities of dreams
Have windows the color of stars?
                                        And who is to say
If the drumbeats we hear at night are real,
                                        or merely those of our hearts?

First visible full moon for months,
                                March already and no snow,
Landscape enlarged and Piranesied back to the east.
Wreckage of water, word rot,
Stanzas in Indian file like cars on a cliff-face dirt road,
The steering wheel in one
                        falling apart in our hands.

Dark birds, we peck at the crumbs of light
Incessantly
                scattered across the stones and hard yard.
An incandescence covers us like a sky, that will
Not comfort us, a brightness
Beyond belief, peck peck,
                        peck peck peck.

On the mountain of Purgatory,
St. Lucy carries the body of Dante up in his sleep,
The stars, as William Blake dreamed,
Hanging like anchorites above them,

The stars, as William Blake perceived them,
                              hard-edged and inconsolable.

Our own dreams lie elsewhere, it seems.
Like junkyard dogs, they rise and loom
              at the ends of their chains, snarling and barking.
We can't get past them.
Who knows what onslaughts they guard,
Detritus or set-asides, hemoglobin perhaps who knows?

BODY AND SOUL II

....

(*for Coleman Hawkins*)

The structure of landscape is infinitesimal,
Like the structure of music,
                              seamless, invisible.
Even the rain has larger sutures.
What holds the landscape together, and what holds music together,
Is faith, it appears—faith of the eye, faith of the ear.
Nothing like that in language,
However, clouds chugging from west to east like blossoms
Blown by the wind.
                    April, and anything's possible.

Here is the story of Hsuan Tsang.
A Buddhist monk, he went from Xian to southern India
And back—on horseback, on camel-back, on elephant-back, and on
    foot.
Ten thousand miles it took him, from 629 to 645,
Mountains and deserts,
In search of the Truth,
                        the heart of the heart of Reality,
The Law that would help him escape it,
And all its attendant and inescapable suffering.
                                        And he found it.

These days, I look at things, not through them,
And sit down low, as far away from the sky as I can get.
The reef of the weeping cherry flourishes coral,
The neighbor's back porch lightbulbs glow like anemones.

Squid-eyed Venus floats forth overhead.
This is the half hour, half-light, half-dark,
                              when everything starts to shine out,
And aphorisms skulk in the trees,
Their wings folded, their heads bowed.

Every true poem is a spark,
                     and aspires to the condition of the original fire
Arising out of the emptiness.
It is that same emptiness it wants to reignite.
It is that same engendering it wants to be re-engendered by.
Shooting stars.
April's identical,
                  celestial, wordless, burning down.
Its light is the light we commune by.
Its destination's our own, its hope is the hope we live with.

Wang Wei, on the other hand,
Before he was 30 years old bought his famous estate on the Wang River
Just east of the east end of the Southern Mountains,
                                        and lived there,
Off and on, for the rest of his life.
He never travelled the landscape, but stayed inside it,
A part of nature himself, he thought.
And who would say no
To someone so bound up in solitude,
                           in failure, he thought, and suffering.

Afternoon sky the color of Cream of Wheat, a small
Dollop of butter hazily at the western edge.
Getting too old and lazy to write poems,
                                  I watch the snowfall
From the apple trees.
Landscape, as Wang Wei says, softens the sharp edges of isolation.

Don't just do something, sit there.
And so I have, so I have,
                    the seasons curling around me like smoke,
Gone to the end of the earth and back without a sound.

NOTES

....

LOOKING AROUND III

Osip Mandelstam, *Selected Poems*, translated by Clarence Brown and W. S. Merwin (1974).

MILDLY DEPRESSED, FAR FROM HOME, I GO OUTSIDE FOR A WHILE

The Jade Mountain, translated by Witter Bynner (1978).

THE SECRET OF POETRY

Wallace Stevens, "Three Travellers Watch a Sunrise," *Opus Posthumous* (1957).

NIGHT RIDER

Roberto Calasso, *Ka*, translated by Tim Parks (1998).

IF MY GLASSES WERE BETTER, I COULD SEE WHERE I'M HEADED FOR

Carter Family, "The Pilgrim Slippers" (trad.).

IS

Annie Dillard, *For the Time Being* (1999).

POLAROIDS

Osip Mandelstam, *Selected Poems*; Georg Trakl, *Poems*, translated by Lucia Getsi (1973).

NIGHT MUSIC

The Jade Mountain; *The Nag Hammadi Library*, James M. Robinson, general editor (1988).

RELICS

Aldo Buzzi, "Notes on Life," *A Weakness for Almost Everything* (1999).

NINE-PANEL YAAK RIVER SCREEN

Georg Trakl, *Poems*; Osip Mandelstam, *Selected Poems*.

BODY AND SOUL II

Richard Bernstein, *Ultimate Journey* (2001).